To: ....

....

From: ....

POSITIVELY POOH

A Book for Students
of All Ages

EGMONT

We bring stories to life

First published in Great Britain 2006 by Egmont UK Limited
239 Kensington High Street, London W8 6SA

Selected text from *WINNIE-THE-POOH* and *THE HOUSE AT POOH CORNER* by A. A. Milne
© The Trustees of the Pooh Properties

Line drawings © E.H. Shepard, colouring © 1970, 1973 and 1974 E.H. Shepard and Egmont UK Ltd

Sketches from THE POOH SKETCHBOOK copyright © 1982 Lloyds TSB Bank PLC
Executors of the Estate of E.H. Shepard, and the E.H. Shepard Trust.

This edition © 2006 The Trustees of the Pooh Properties

Book design and new text © 2006 Egmont UK Ltd
Text by Emily Stead and Janette Marshall

ISBN 1 4052 2386 3
ISBN 978 1 4052 2386 7

3 5 7 9 10 8 6 4 2
Printed and bound in Malaysia

A CIP catalogue record for this title is available from the British Library

POSITIVELY POOH

A Book for Students of All Ages

A.A. Milne

Illustrated by E.H. Shepard

EGMONT

'You ought to write "A Happy Birthday" on it.'
'That was what I wanted to ask you,' said Pooh.
'Because my spelling is Wobbly. It's good spelling
but it Wobbles, and the letters get in the wrong places.
Would you write "A Happy Birthday" on it for me?' . .
So Owl wrote . . . and this is what he wrote:

HIPY PAPY BTHUTHDTH THUTHDA BTHUTHD

Pooh looked on admiringly.
'I'm just saying "A Happy Birthday",' said Owl carelessly.
'It's a nice long one,' said Pooh, very much impressed by it.
'Well, actually, of course, I'm saying "A very Happy
Birthday with love from Pooh." Naturally it takes a
good deal of pencil to say a long thing like that.'
'Oh, I see,' said Pooh.

Invest in a good dictionary

Essay? What essay?

'I *think*,' said Piglet, when he had licked the tip of his nose too, and found that it brought very little comfort, 'I *think* that I have just remembered something. I have just remembered something that I forgot to do yesterday and shan't be able to do to-morrow. So I suppose I really ought to go back and do it now.'

'We'll do it this afternoon, and I'll come with you,' said Pooh.

'It isn't the sort of thing you can do in the afternoon,' said Piglet quickly. 'It's a very particular morning thing, that has to be done in the morning, and, if possible, tween the hours of – What would you say the time was?'

About twelve,' said Winnie-the-Pooh, looking at the sun. Between, as I was saying, the hours of twelve and twelve five. So, really, dear old Pooh, if you'll excuse me . . .'

Don't be bamboozled by jargon

'Well,' said Owl, 'the customary procedure
in such cases is as follows.'
'What does Crustimoney Proseedcake mean?'
said Pooh. 'For I am a Bear of Very Little Brain,
and long words Bother me.'
'It means the Thing to Do.'
'As long as it means that, I don't mind,'
said Pooh humbly.

'Oh, Pooh Bear, what shall we do?'
And then this Bear, Pooh Bear,
Winnie-the-Pooh, F.O.P. (Friend of Piglet's),
R.C. (Rabbit's Companion), P.D. (Pole Discoverer),
E.C. and T.F. (Eeyore's Comforter and Tail-finder) –
in fact, Pooh himself – said something so clever
that Christopher Robin could only look at him
with mouth open and eyes staring, wondering
if this was really the Bear of Very Little Brain
whom he had known and loved so long.

ne day you'll have impressive
initials after your name too!

Parents have their uses

Now it happened that Kanga had felt rather motherly that morning, and Wanting to Count Things – like Roo's vests, and how many pieces of soap there were left, and the two clean spots in Tigger's feeder; so she had sent them out with a packet of watercress sandwiches for Roo and a packet of extract-of-malt sandwiches for Tigger, to have a nice long morning in the forest not getting into mischief. And off they had gone.

'After all,' said Rabbit to himself
'Christopher Robin depends on Me.
He's fond of Pooh and Piglet and
Eeyore, and so am I, but they
haven't any Brain. Not to notice.
And he respects Owl, because
you can't help respecting anybody
who can spell TUESDAY,
even if he doesn't spell it right;
but spelling isn't everything.
There are days when spelling
Tuesday simply doesn't count.

Spelling isn't everything

Remember the purpose of those early-morning lectures

GON OUT
BACKSON
BISY
BACKSON
C.R.

'There's just one thing I wanted to ask you,
Eeyore. What happens to Christopher Robin
in the mornings nowadays?' . . .
'What does Christopher Robin do in the mornings?
He learns. He becomes Educated. He instigorates –
I *think* that is the word he mentioned, but I may be
eferring to something else – he instigorates Knowledge.

xt morning the notice on Christopher Robin's door said:

GONE OUT
BACK SOON
C.R.

Get used to the parties

'Owl,' said Christopher Robin, 'I am going to give a part

'You are, are you?' said Owl.

'And it's to be a special sort of party, because
it's because of what Pooh did when he did what
he did to save Piglet from the flood.'

'Oh, that's what it's for, is it?' said Owl.

'Yes, so will you tell Pooh as quickly as you can,
and all the others, because it will be to-morrow?'

'Oh, it will, will it?' said Owl, still being
as helpful as possible.

'So will you go and tell them, Owl?'

Owl tried to think of something very wise to say,
but couldn't, so he flew off to tell the others.

And the first person he told was Pooh.

Some of the best fun
in life is free

Kanga and Roo were spending a quiet afternoon in a sandy part of the Forest. Baby Roo was practising very small jumps in the sand, and falling down mouse-holes and climbing out of them, and Kanga was fidgeting about and saying 'Just one more jump, dear, and then we must go home.' And at that moment who should come stumping up the hill but Pooh.

'Good afternoon, Kanga.'

'Good afternoon, Pooh.'

'Look at me jumping,' squeaked Roo, and fell into another mouse-hole.

How organdized are you?

'Now,' said Rabbit, 'this is a Search,
and I've Organized it –'
'Done what to it?' said Pooh.
'Organized it. Which means – well, it's what you do to
a Search, when you don't all look in the same place
at once. So I want *you*, Pooh, to search by the Six Pine
Trees first, and then work your way towards Owl's Hous
and look out for me there. Do you see?'
'No,' said Pooh. 'What –'
'Then I'll see you at Owl's House in about an hour's tim
'Is Piglet organdized too?'
'We all are,' said Rabbit, and off he went.

Hospitable students make friends easily

The sun was so delightfully warm, and the stone,
which had been sitting in it for a long time,
was so warm, too, that Pooh had almost decided to
go on being Pooh in the middle of the stream for the
rest of the morning, when he remembered Rabbit.
'Rabbit,' said Pooh to himself.
'I *like* talking to Rabbit. He talks about sensible things.
He doesn't use long, difficult words, like Owl.
He uses short, easy words, like "What about lunch?"
and "Help yourself, Pooh." I suppose, *really*,
ought to go and see Rabbit.'

Allow enough time for a morning wash!

Roo was washing his face and paws
in the stream, while Kanga explained to everybody
proudly that this was the first time he had ever
washed his face himself, and Owl was telling
Kanga an Interesting Anecdote full of long words
like Encyclopaedia and Rhododendron to
which Kanga wasn't listening.
'I don't hold with all this washing,' grumbled Eeyore.
'This modern Behind-the-ears nonsense.
What do *you* think, Pooh?'

Be welcoming to new student

'What I don't like about it is this,' said Rabbit.
'Here are we – you, Pooh, and you, Piglet,
and Me – and suddenly –'
'And Eeyore,' said Pooh.
'And, Eeyore – and then suddenly –'
'And Owl,' said Pooh.
'And Owl – and then all of a sudden –'
'Oh, and Eeyore,' said Pooh. 'I was forgetting *him*.'
'Here – we – are,' said Rabbit very slowly and carefully,
'l – of – us, and then, suddenly, we wake up one morning,
d what do we find? We find a Strange Animal among us.
An animal of whom we had never even heard before!'

'You bounced me,' said Eeyore gruffly.

'I didn't really. I had a cough, and I happened to be behind Eeyore, and I said "*Grr-oppp-ptschschschz*."'

'Why?' said Rabbit, helping Piglet up, and dusting him. 'It's all right, Piglet.'

'It took me by surprise,' said Piglet nervously.

'That's what I call bouncing,' said Eeyore. 'Taking people by surprise. Very unpleasant habit. I don't mind Tigger being in the Forest,' he went on, 'because it's a large Forest, and there's plenty of room to bounce in it. But I don't see why he should come into *my* little corner of it, and bounce there.'

Respect other people's space

Find a balance of
work and play

'I might have known,' said Eeyore.
'After all, one can't complain. I have my friends.
Somebody spoke to me only yesterday. And was
it last week or the week before that Rabbit
bumped into me and said "Bother!"
The Social Round. Always something going on.'

Take a break to avoid
making mistakes

[Pooh] was so tired when he got home that,
in the very middle of his supper, after he had
been eating for little more than half-an-hour, he fell
fast asleep in his chair, and slept and slept and slept.

So he took his largest pot of honey and escaped
with it to a broad branch of his tree,
well above the water, and then he climbed
down again and escaped with another pot . . .
and when the whole Escape was finished,
there was Pooh sitting on his branch,
dangling his legs, and there, beside him,
were ten pots of honey . . .

Two days later, there was Pooh,
sitting on his branch, dangling his legs,
and there beside him, were four pots
of honey. Three days later, there was Pooh,
sitting on his branch, dangling his legs,
and there beside him, was one pot of honey.

Are you getting a nutritious, balanced diet?

*Enlist your friends'
help when
house-hunting . . .*

Pooh had had a Mysterious Missage
underneath his front door that morning, saying,

'I AM SCERCHING FOR
A NEW HOUSE FOR OWL
SO HAD YOU RABBIT,'

and while he was wondering what it meant
Rabbit had come in and read it for him.
'I'm leaving one for all the others,' said Rabbit,
'and telling them what it means,
and they'll all search too.
I'm in a hurry, good-bye.'

...And choose your accommodation wisely

Pooh had wandered into the
Hundred Acre Wood, and was
standing in front of what had
once been Owl's House. It didn't
look at all like a house now;
it looked like a tree which had
been blown down; and as soon as
a house looks like that, it is time
you tried to find another one.

Even party animals need their beauty sleep

So Whatever-it-was came here, and in the light
of the candle he and Pooh looked at each other.
'I'm Pooh,' said Pooh.
'I'm Tigger,' said Tigger.
'Oh!' said Pooh, for he had never seen an animal like this
before. 'Does Christopher Robin know about you?'
'Of course he does,' said Tigger.
'Well,' said Pooh, 'it's the middle of the night,
which is a good time for going to sleep.
And to-morrow morning we'll have some
honey for breakfast. Do Tiggers like honey?'
'They like everything,' said Tigger cheerfully.
'Then if they like going to sleep on the floor,
I'll go back to bed,' said Pooh, 'and we'll do things
in the morning. Good night.'

'Let's have a look at you.'

So Eeyore stood there, gazing sadly at the ground, and Winnie-the-Pooh walked all round him once.

'Why, what's happened to your tail?' he said in surprise.

'What *has* happened to it?' said Eeyore.

'It isn't there!'

'Are you sure?'

'Well, either a tail *is* there or it isn't there. You can't make a mistake about it, and yours *isn't* there.'

'Then what is?'

'Nothing.'

When did you last have
a thorough check-up?

Keep an eye on your friends' welfare too

'I don't know how it is, Christopher Robin, but what
with all this snow and one thing and another, not to
mention icicles and such-like, it isn't so Hot in my field
about three o'clock in the morning as some people think
it is. It isn't Close, if you know what I mean – not so as
to be uncomfortable. It isn't Stuffy. In fact, Christopher
Robin,' he went on in a loud whisper, 'quite-between-
ourselves-and-don't-tell-anybody, it's Cold.'
'Oh, Eeyore!'

Sometimes appointments are necessary

One day when Pooh Bear had nothing else to do, he thought he would do something, so he went round to Piglet's house to see what Piglet was doing. It was still snowing as he stumped over the white forest track, and he expected to find Piglet warming his toes in front of his fire, but to his surprise he saw that the door was open, and the more he looked inside the more Piglet wasn't there.

'He's out,' said Pooh sadly. 'That's what it is. He's not in.'

Do your presentation skills need work?

'If anybody wants to clap,' said Eeyore when
he had read this, 'now is the time to do it.'
They all clapped.
'Thank you,' said Eeyore.
'Unexpected and gratifying, if a little lacking in Smack.'

They had got a rope and were pulling Owl's chairs and pictures and things out of his old house so as to be ready to put them into his new one. Kanga was down below tying the things on, and calling out to Owl, 'You won't want this dirty old dish-cloth any more, will you, and what about this carpet, it's all in holes,' and Owl was calling back indignantly, 'Of course I do! It's just a question of arranging the furniture properly, and it isn't a dish-cloth, it's my shawl.'

Don't question others'
fashion fauxs pas

No idea is a bad idea

'I've got a sort of idea,' said Pooh at last,
'but I don't suppose it's a very good one.'
'I don't suppose it is either,' said Eeyore.
'Go on, Pooh,' said Rabbit. 'Let's have it.'
'Well, if we all threw stones and things into
the river on *one* side of Eeyore, the stones
would make waves, and the waves would
wash him to the other side.'
'That's a very good idea,' said Rabbit,
and Pooh looked happy again.

Bachelor of Philosophy?

The Old Grey Donkey, Eeyore, stood by himself
in a thistly corner of the Forest, his front feet well apar
his head on one side, and thought about things. Sometin
he thought sadly to himself, 'Why?' and sometimes he
thought, 'Wherefore?' and sometimes he thought,
'Inasmuch as which?' – and sometimes
he didn't quite know what he *was* thinking about.

Research your subject
thoroughly

'I saw a Heffalump to-day, Piglet.'
'What was it doing?' asked Piglet.
'Just lumping along,' said Christopher Robin.
'I don't think it saw *me*.'
'I saw one once,' said Piglet. 'At least,
I think I did,' he said. 'Only perhaps it wasn't.'
'So did I,' said Pooh, wondering
what a Heffalump was like.

Teamwork is a useful skill

'I have decided to catch a Heffalump.'
Pooh nodded his head several times as he said this,
and waited for Piglet to say 'How?' or 'Pooh,
you couldn't!' or something helpful of that sort,
but Piglet said nothing. The fact was Piglet
was wishing that *he* had thought about it first.
'I shall do it,' said Pooh, after waiting a little longer,
'by means of a trap. And it must be a Cunning Trap,
so you will have to help me, Piglet.'
'Pooh,' said Piglet, feeling quite happy again now,
'I will.' And then he said, 'How shall we do it?'
and Pooh said, 'That's just it. How?'
And then they sat down together to think it out.

You need never
stop learning

Suddenly Christopher Robin began to tell Pooh about some of the things: People called Kings and Queens and something called Factors, and a place called Europe, and an island in the middle of the sea where no ships came, and how you make a Suction Pump (if you want to), and when Knights were Knighted, and what comes from Brazil. And Pooh, his back against one of the sixty-something trees, and his paws folded in front of him, said 'Oh!' and 'I don't know,' and thought how wonderful it would be to have a Real Brain which could tell you things. And by-and-by Christopher Robin came to an end of the things, and was silent, and he sat there looking out over the world, and wishing it wouldn't stop.